A Quilter's Tale

A personal collection of colourful quilts & quilting.

Rosemary Marozzi

Dedication

I dedicate this little book to my three children Belinda, Justin and Isabella and also to my daughter in law Julia, whose idea it was to have all the quilts photographed and catalogued.

Thank you all so much for being there for me.

This is also an opportunity to thank my fellow quilters for their support and advice and who after many years have become dear friends. It has been a privilege to be in such a lovely group of people where we have been able to share all our highs and lows. Above all, the laughter has been a huge tonic!

Thank you girls.

Thanks also to Mel, Lizzi and Jimmy, who have together contributed so much to the making of this book - for the photography, technical skills and ideas for the presentation etc. Your patience and vision were an inspiration.

Photography by Mel Smith at Rose Farm Studio, Pluckley, Kent.

Contents

Introduction

If you are reading this (or have picked up this book), you are probably either a family member or a keen quilter! Perhaps you have taken up quilting as a hobby in later years or been inspired by a quilter you have met at some point.

For me, it was a back operation and subsequent convalescence in 1981 which propelled me into the world of quilting. I have my mother to thank for this as one morning she arrived with a little BBC booklet which opened my eyes to an exciting world of American quilting. I was entranced by the beautiful quilts, cushions, and clothing which I'd never seen before.

I could not wait to begin to make some of these lovely things myself. I was initially captivated by the log cabin form of patchwork. As soon as I was up and about again, I began with making different blocks. My husband quickly noticed that the only time I was not complaining about my back was when I was sitting at my sewing machine making piles of blocks!

Quite quickly (with the help of my mother), I managed to produce 4 queen-sized quilts all made in Liberty's Tana Lawns.

Without my knowledge, my husband (always a businessman) made an appointment with the buyer of Liberty's bedding department. After I had got over the shock, we struggled up to London with the 4 quilts and 10 cushions. The buyer took the lot!

Then began the busy years of producing large American style quilts and supplying Liberty's, Harrods and other smaller specialist shops. My back problems reduced and life was busy and productive.

I then had to enlist the help of some local ladies and suddenly a small cottage industry was born. As well as quilts and cushions, I was later able to supply Liberty's with knitting bags and waistcoats, all in their Tana Lawns.

Later, I met and joined a group of Canterbury quilters (the Chaucer Quilters) and together we made quilts for exhibitions as well as for various charities. In about 1987, I opened a small quilt shop in the converted stables of my home. Later, of course, my friends all asked me to teach them, and there were several years of giving classes in the studio, with lunches in the house where I had to brush up my cooking skills!

There was a great interest in England for quilting, but it was still difficult to find quilting shops. I was fortunate that people living in my area and of course friends, supported my small business and I even had a few customers from across the channel.

As you will see, I have arranged this book in three sections spanning a period of around 35 years.

Section 1
The Early Years - The Liberty Connection

Section 2
The Baltimore Style and Appliqué Quilts

Section 3
The Small Antique Quilt Collection

As you may understand, a vast amount of work that I have produced has been sold, but this is what remains. As with all artistic collections, there is a life story behind the progression of exhibits. This has a significance which I would not want to go unspoken. Please read not only the introduction to each section but also the accompanying text.

Above all, I hope you will find the quilts themselves both interesting and inspiring in both their subject matter and their progression.

October 2017

The Early Years
&
The Liberty Connection

At the first exhibition of quilts held in the Chapter House of Canterbury Cathedral in 1985. Here I am with my father, Rolf Barham, and youngest daughter Isabella.

The blue log cabin quilt on the right hand side of the picture was like one of many sold at Liberty's in London over several years.

Patchwork Jacket

This jacket was made in preparation for the opening of the quilt exhibition in the Chapter House of Canterbury Cathedral in 1985, where I had to greet the Mayor!

The jacket was made up of many blue shades of Tana Lawn fabric from Liberty's.

1985

A Sampler Quilt for Belinda

My first Sampler Quilt made together with my
mother, for my daughter Belinda's 21st birthday.

She never took delivery of it and over the years, it
became a great teaching tool for my students!

1985

Rose of Sharon Quilt

This king-sized machine appliqué quilt in Tana
Lawn was made for an exhibition in Liberty's.

My father who had watched me making it didn't
want me to let it go. When he died rather suddenly,
I asked Liberty's if I could have it back.

Am still waiting to quilt it!

1986/7

A King-Sized Kaleidoscope Quilt

I made this large quilt in Tana Lawn for Liberty's
but never got round to delivering it to them.

It has finally gone to my son Justin, whose wife
Julia loved the colours.

1986/7

14

Kaleidoscope Quilt

Another large quilt for Liberty's and the same popular design, this time in pink and red colours.

1986/7

A Quilt for Mother

I made a single-bed sized quilt for my mother,
'Ging', in this Liberty Tana Lawn print, and she
loved it.

It went with her to the retirement home near us
and later covered her coffin at her funeral.

1988

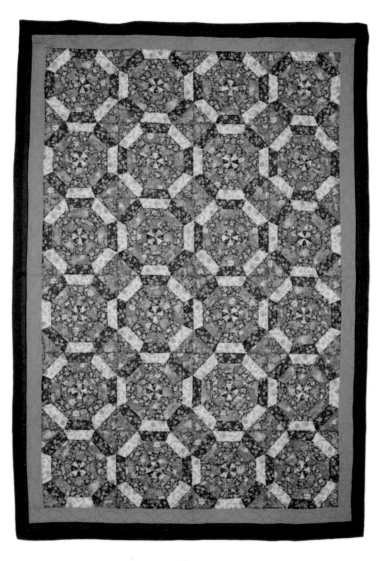

Kaleidoscope Quilt Sample

Whenever I was teaching, I would pin up a small
quilt sample on the pinboard.

This is one of them, and this design proved to be
very popular with the students.

1987/8

A Quilt for Cambridge

A kaleidoscope quilt design made as a surprise for
my son Justin, who was returning from overseas
before going on to university.

I was initially horrified when I found it was being
used as a draft excluder in his room! Later, he did
hang it properly.

1989

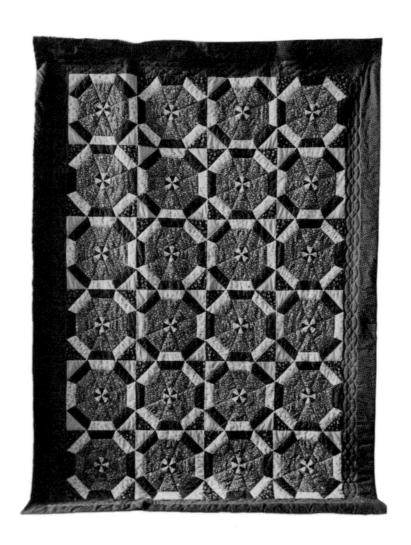

Jacket Sample

This was a sample made for a class I was teaching
on patchwork jackets.

They were always a great success and fun to do.

1993

A Summer Workshop

Here is a group of my students who had all been
busy making patchwork jackets.

Seen here outside the studio after a large lunch in
the garden.

1990

Pearl Wedding Quilt

When in Paducah in the States in 1989, I bought a
whole cloth quilt top already marked up.

The fabric was fine American lawn and I used silk
for the bows and binding.

It took four months to complete.

Everyone loves it.

1989

Sales Item

One last remaining log-cabin knitting bag out of
the many sold to Liberty's in London over several
years.

1990

The Baltimore and Appliqué Style Quilts

Around 1994 and 1995, I went on a Baltimore Album quilting course in Lancashire and fell in love with this type of quilting.

A short time later, I had an unexpected and dramatic 'Damascus Road' experience which changed my life, and also my quilts. The quality became noticeably higher. I then discovered that the early Baltimore quilts made between 1840 and 1860 were all based on Christianity and were often made for visiting and departing ministers of the Gospel. Each flower, leaf, stem etc. were all different symbols of the Gospel story.

The Parkinson's Quilt

This quilt was made by the Chaucer quilters and
was offered as a raffle prize for the Parkinson's
disease society.

It helped raise £120,000. It was won by a man of 90
who rang me to say he was putting his twin beds
together in order to use the quilt.

1989

The Cherub Quilt

A group quilt made by the Chaucer Quilters.

Fun to make and a challenge to do the cherubs,
which are difficult to see in the photograph.

It was raffled for charity.

Blocks designed by Patricia Cox.

1998/9

The Tulip Quilt

This quilt was made from a pattern bought at a
quilt show.

It was an easy pattern but it used bondaweb, which
I didn't like.

It is still waiting to be quilted!

1990

A Hint of Baltimore

This large quilt comprising several quilted borders
with a central medallion panel of appliquéd flowers
was made in memory of my mother.

It was later displayed in the marquee at my
daughter Belinda's wedding in 1994.

1993

To God Be The Glory

This is my first Baltimore album quilt made over two years following a quilting course in Preston, Lancashire in 1993.

It was to be the start of a great love for this type of appliqué work.

The title was the result of an unexpected conversion in June 1994.

1994/5

The Flowers of the Field

Much of this quilt was made whilst sitting at my
husband's bedside in hospital.

I made 135 different flowers, all examples of God's
wonderful creation.

It took fifteen months to complete.

"Men are like grass and the flowers of the field:
they wither and die... But God's love is from
everlasting to everlasting."

2001

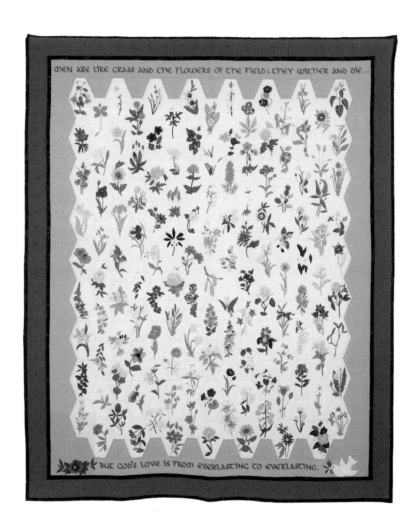

Teaching Blocks Quilt

This quilt was made out of my former teaching
samples.

I made a large medallion block for the centre.

The fabrics now look very dated!

1997

Clementine's Quilt

I decided to make my 9 year old granddaughter
Clem a quilt as a surprise.

I chose an Amish style quilt design using plainish
colours and sample blocks of trees and houses.

The verse on the lower border seemed very
appropriate and she told me later she loved the
writing best of all.

"In my Father's house there are many mansions."

1996

Small Baltimore Panel

This circular floral border incorporates all the techniques needed to make a Baltimore quilt and was a very useful teaching tool for my students.

One of my best designs.

1996/7

Song of Solomon

This quilt, designed by me, but owned by
Joan Poole, was made by the Chaucer Quilters
in 1997.

One of our first group quilts, which we all enjoyed
making.

1997

The Fruit of The Spirit

This quilt, designed and owned by me, was made
by the 10 members of the Chaucer Quilters in
1997.

It took 10 quilters 1 year to make this quilt from
start to finish, and at 9' square, it is the largest of all
the quilts.

It was later displayed during the Millennium and
was viewed by the Archbishop of Canterbury.

"Let not your hearts be troubled and do not be
afraid."

"Seek Me and you will find Me when you seek Me
with all your heart."

"Lo, I am with you always even unto the end of
the world."

"Come unto Me all who are weary and heavy laden
and I will give you rest. "

1997

The Fruit of The Spirit

Seen here at Sandown Park Quilt Championships
are 6 members of the Chaucer Quilters who
contributed to making this quilt.

It was awarded a rosette.

From left to right they are:

Barbara Grayson, Trudy Smethurst,
Marion Collins, Rosemary Marozzi, Joan Poole
and Sue Homan

The Parrot Quilt

One of the Chaucer Quilters came back from a
holiday in Florida and gave each of us a small piece
of black and green leaf fabric with parrots amongst
the leaves from which we each made a small quilt.
It was amazing how different all the 8 quilts turned
out to be.

They were later taken to Germany for an
exhibition near Hanover.

2004

The Miniature Quilt

Years before we had quilt shops selling wonderful fabric, we had to use mail-order companies. They would send out one-inch squares of assorted materials.

This quilt is the result of using up those little samples.

2004

The Gospel According to
St. Luke

I had for a long time intended making a brightly
coloured Biblical quilt with some of the stories of
the Old Testament, but somehow it turned into the
Gospel story!

This is probably my most challenging piece of
work. It took 2 years to complete less 4 months for
the drawings.

2005/7

The Celtic Goose Quilt

I had made the Celtic goose as a centrepiece for a
friend's quilt. It turned out to be too small, so I
made her a larger one and kept this one for myself.

I found out later the Celtic goose is a symbol of the
Holy Spirit.

I enjoyed making this small quilt but it was
considerably complicated!

2003

The Country Ways Quilt

A small quilt made using different blocks and
designs which I'd always fancied making.

It was difficult to put together and, too late, I
realised I should have used graph paper!

This quilt seems to be everyone's favourite.

2008

Sugar and Spice
& All Things Nice

My first attempt at a Strippy quilt and great fun to
do. I love the 'flea market' fabrics and the designs
came from a child's colouring book.

"I have called you by name." (Isaiah : 43:1)

2009

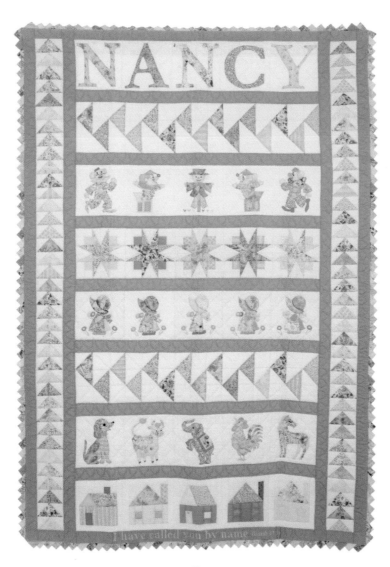

The Dinosaur Quilt

I found the dinosaur designs on some of my
grandson William's playing cards.

This was a small quilt to fit his bunk bed. The verse
fitted very conveniently into the lower border.

"I will never leave you nor forsake you."
(Joshua : 1:5)

2009

The Flower Fairy Quilt

My granddaughter, Iris, asked me for a quilt with
fairies, mushrooms and stars. This is what she got
and I loved making it.

A lot of embroidery was needed and the faces were
a great challenge.

Verse on the back reads

"Jesus said, let the little children come unto me."
(Matthew : 19:14)

2010

Japan - Lest We Forget

I found this pattern in a French quilting magazine and loved using the different fabrics. The challenge was to fit it all together.

The quilt was finished at about the time of the Japanese tsunami and nuclear explosions - hence the title.

The verse on the back reads
"Daisy, 'Lo, I am with you always, even unto the end of the World.'"

2011

The Chaucer Quilters'
'Magnum Opus'

When sorting out my old patterns, I gave my
fellow quilters three patterns each and asked them
to make me a block for a joint quilt project. This is
the result.

It took nearly four years to complete and we all
love it. We can't decide who should have it or
where it should go.

2012/14

Jellyroll Quilt

This is a stab at a Jellyroll quilt. As the fabrics are
pre-cut, it seems a bit of a cheat.

Pretty quick to do and no initiative needed!

2012

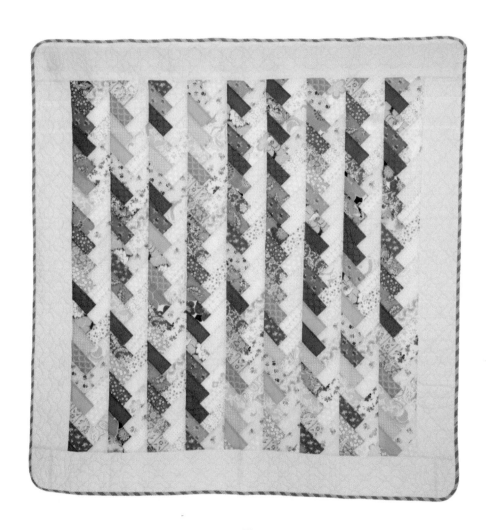

"Vanity, Vanity, All is Vanity"

A card from a friend (2nd hat down on the left)
inspired me to make a quilt of 1930s hats.

When I was halfway through it, my son Justin was
kidnapped in Libya and it was quilting which
helped to calm me down. I made the 2nd hat down
on the right during this time, and it has become my
favourite.

Happily, my son was released just before it was
finished.

2012

Unfinished Symphony

I had planned for this to be a large Baltimore quilt,
but this centrepiece ended up as a small quilt
instead.

I enjoyed putting cherubs in amongst the flowers
and beading the border.

"My peace I give unto you."
(John : 14:27)

2013

Lanterns and Stars Quilt - A Family Affair

A friend gave me a copy of this design and I loved making this quilt. I decided to use up some of my lovely Liberty fabrics.

I then went on holiday to France where I enlisted the help of 3 of my grandchildren to make some of the blocks. They did a great job. They were William and Iris (both 9) and Nancy (6).

"Narrow is the way that leads to life, and few there be that find it." (Matthew : 7:14)

2013

'Narrow is the way that leads to life and few there be that find it.' [Matt 7:14]

The 12 Days of Christmas

I borrowed this pattern from a friend whose quilt I
admired.

I thoroughly enjoyed making it.

"Be joyful always."
(Phil. : 4:4)

2014

A Christmas Hanging

This Christmas hanging proved to be FAR more work than I had anticipated. The family expected more 'toys' in the pockets but I insisted it was not an advent calendar.

Nobody wants it!

2016

The Lord's Prayer Quilt

I had great pleasure making the different appliqué blocks, mostly designed by Margaret Docherty and Shirley Bloomfield.

They were done using my favourite colours. The text was added later.

Fifteen months to complete.

2016

The Lord's Prayer

Our Father, who art in heaven, hallowed be thy name.
Thy kingdom come, Thy will be done, on earth as it is in heaven...

The Bird Quilt

I found a bird book amongst my quilting books,
which I had bought 15 years ago and decided to
make a quilt from some of the patterns inside.

The piecing was fairly complicated.

The verse added later is:

"Look at the birds, they neither plant or harvest or
put food in barns because your heavenly Father
feeds them, and you are far more valuable to Him
than they are."
(Matthew : 6:26)

2017

A Christmas Table Runner

Following the Lantern and Stars design of a recent
quilt, I decided to make the table runner.

A very simple project for once!

2015

The Antique Quilt Collection

The following quilts were collected by my husband and me over several trips to America. We used to go to Houston where a large wholesale market took place 3 days before the main exhibition of quilts and this is where we found several quilt treasures.

The Strip-String Quilt

Bought in America on a trip to Houston, Texas
where my husband and I had gone to attend the
wholesale quilt market.

This quilt is simple and rather roughly made but
has a character all of its own.

1930s

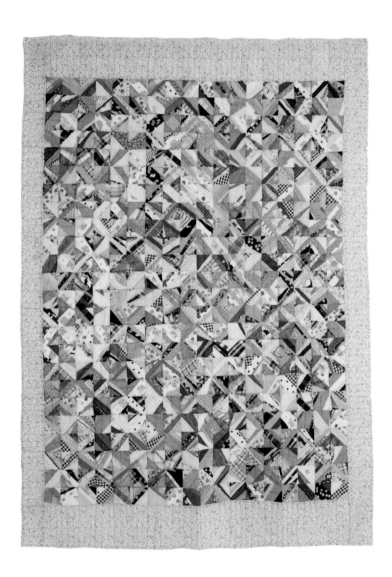

The Postage Stamp Quilt

Bought in America in 1986 in Houston, Texas. A
scrap quilt with tiny piecing and rather heavy.

1930s

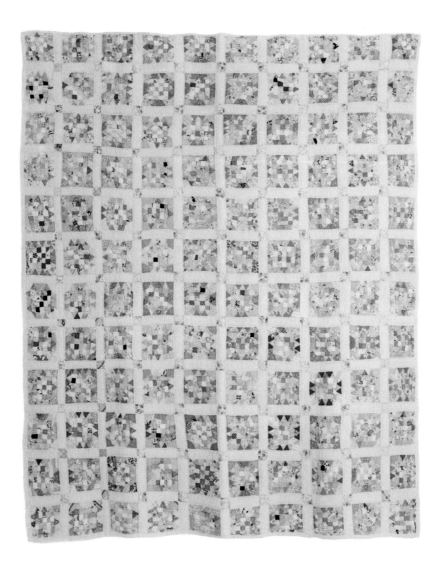

Trip Around the World Quilt

This is a well-known design and a favourite quilt of mine. It was bought in Houston in 1986.

It had an accident of black ink being spilled on it. I was so shocked by this that it took 15 years before I could face attempting the repair!

Can you see the 4 inserted new fabrics?

1930s

The Diamond Quilt

Whilst in Houston, my husband and I found this
quilt in a quilt shop, but it was not for sale. One
and a half hours later, my husband walked out of
the shop with the quilt under his arm, having
persuaded the owner to part with it!

It is a masterpiece and I would love to know how
long it took to make.

1930s

Rose of Sharon Quilt

This is a much loved traditional design, and in this
case, it may even have been a quilt kit. It is always
lovely to look at.

However, this quilt would not keep anyone warm.
There's no wadding inside at all.

1930s

Double Irish Chain Quilt

This is a scrap quilt and a very popular design.

It is now owned by my great niece, Lily, and looks
lovely on her brass bed.

1930s

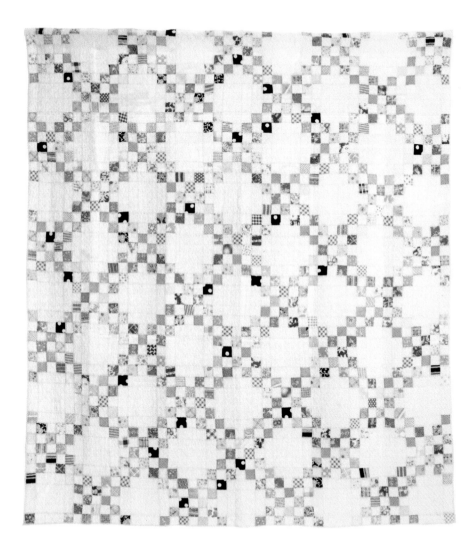

The Dogwood Quilt

A quilt I bought literally as I was just leaving for
my plane home.

The Dogwood flowers in the spring and is seen in
the Midwest, which I was visiting (in Paducah).

This could even have been a quilt kit. This is a
pretty and romantic little quilt and although the
fabric has become old and worn, it feels like silk.
I just love it!

1930s

The 1840 Quilt
Rose Wreath Design

This is one of a pair and I have used both quilts on
my twin beds for many years.

The rose fabric rotted and I had to replace all the
red flowers with magenta coloured fabric. I also
took the opportunity to add on a narrow border all
around the quilts as they were so narrow.

1840

The Melon Quilt

This was a very shabby quilt top lying under a
table in a quilt shop in Houston. I bought it very
cheaply and years later, when I began to quilt it, I
discovered there were many patches that needed
replacing.

It was hard to find appropriate fabrics for this
1930s quilt.

1930s

Double Wedding Ring Quilt

This was just a very frail-looking quilt top which I found in a basket at a quilt show in America. It was many years before I got around to quilting it.

The verse on the back reads

'Those whom God hath joined, let no man put asunder.'

Quilted up in 2013.

1930s

The Blue Patchwork Quilt

A scrap patchwork top bought in America at a
quilt show. It is made up of a series of plain and
floral squares as borders. I had to add an outside
border and then quilt it up in 2013.

1930s

The Patchwork Quilt
(Campbell Taylor)

This little picture of a quilter working (about 200 years ago) was given to me one Christmas by my daughter Isabella.

The Last Stitch

Following the preceding photography, I thought it
might be an amusing idea to have a picture of me
finishing the flower quilt 200 years later!

Rosemary Marozzi

Rosemary says she cannot remember a time when there wasn't a needle in her hand, either a knitting or a sewing one.

She learned embroidery in Italy sitting in a humble cottage with an earth floor.

Then came years of dress making and upholstery, and 45 years of collecting old and antique furniture, which became a passion.

It has continued to be a very fulfilled and happy life where she can see God's hand in it all the way through.

Printed in Great Britain
by Amazon